GWINNETT COUNTY PUBLIC LIBRARY FEB - - 2012

DISCARD

D1171144

Fabulous FASHIONs of the 1990s

Felicia Lowenstein
NIVEN

Fabulous FASHIONs of the DECADES

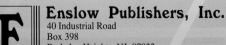

E **Enslow Publishers, Inc.**
40 Industrial Road
Box 398
Berkeley Heights, NJ 07922
USA

http://www.enslow.com

Copyright © 2012 by Felicia Lowenstein Niven

All rights reserved.

No part of this book may be reproduced by any means
without the written permission of the publisher.

Library of Congress Cataloging-in-Publication Data

Niven, Felicia Lowenstein.
    Fabulous fashions of the 1990s / Felicia Lowenstein Niven.
        p. cm. — (Fabulous fashions of the decades)
    Fabulous fashions of the nineteen nineties
    Includes bibliographical references and index.
        Summary: "Discusses the fashions of the 1990s, including women's and men's clothing and hairstyles,
accessories, trends and fads, and world events that influenced the fashion"—Provided by publisher.
        ISBN 978-0-7660-3827-1
        1. Fashion—History—20th century—Juvenile literature. 2. Fashion design—History—20th century—
Juvenile literature. 3. Lifestyle—History—20th century—Juvenile literature. 4. Nineteen nineties—
Juvenile literature. I. Title. II. Title: Fabulous fashions of the nineteen nineties.
    TT504.N583 2011
    746.43'2—dc22
                                                                    2010014590
Paperback ISBN: 978-1-59845-282-2

Printed in the United States of America

052011 Lake Book Manufacturing, Inc., Melrose Park, IL

10 9 8 7 6 5 4 3 2 1

To Our Readers: We have done our best to make sure all Internet Addresses in this book
were active and appropriate when we went to press. However, the author and the publisher have no
control over and assume no liability for the material available on those Internet sites or on other Web
sites they may link to. Any comments or suggestions can be sent by e-mail to comments@enslow.com
or to the address on the back cover.

Every effort has been made to locate all copyright holders of material used in this book. If any errors
or omissions have occurred, corrections will be made in future editions of this book.

♻ Enslow Publishers, Inc., is committed to printing our books on recycled paper. The paper in every
book contains 10% to 30% post-consumer waste (PCW). The cover board on the outside of each book
contains 100% PCW. Our goal is to do our part to help young people and the environment too!

Illustration Credits: AFP/Getty Images, p. 34; AP Images/Jockel Finck, p. 42; AP Images/New Haven Register,
Vern Williams, p. 26; AP Images/Rene Macura, p. 14; BEImages/Rex USA, p. 30; © Bunim-Murray Productions/
courtesy Everett Collection, p. 40; Corel Corporation, p. 47; courtesy Everett Collection, pp. 9, 12, 18, 32, 33;
FilmMagic/Getty Images, p. 17; Library of Congress, pp. 43–45; Mary Evans/Warner Bros./Ronald Grant/Everett
Collection, p. 7; © Michael Newman/PhotoEdit, p. 22; Mirrorpix/courtesy Everett Collection, pp. 8, 24, 35; Nils
Jorgensen/Rex USA, courtesy Everett Collection, p. 13; Peter Brooker/Rex USA/courtesy Everett Collection,
p. 23; © RewareVintage.com, p. 6; Rex Features/courtesy Everett Collection, p. 28; Shutterstock, pp. 1, 4, 10, 15,
20, 21, 25, 27, 29, 31, 36, 37, 39; Starstock/Photoshot/Everett Collection, p. 19.

Cover Illustration: Shutterstock (woman in overalls).

Contents

The 1990s

The 1990s

Wild and Crazy Fads

A shirt that changes color sounds like it belongs in the future. But it actually appeared in the past, in the 1990s. Hypercolor T-shirts were cotton shirts that were treated with a special pigment that reacted to heat. When the fabric got hot, the shirt changed color.

It was a good idea in theory. It was even fun to see the shirt change color. But when you sweated in gym class, it was more than a little embarrassing to see it in living color on your shirt!

If the hypercolor shirt sounds a little crazy, then the next fad of the 1990s was downright wild. The catsuit first appeared back in the sixties as a featured outfit in the popular TV show *The Avengers*. It was not a suit for a cat, but a skintight bodysuit for a woman.

The catsuit appeared again in the 1992 film *Batman Returns*. It was worn by actress Michelle Pfeiffer, who

The heat from this person's hands made the purple hypercolor shirt turn pink!

played Catwoman. The one-piece, form-fitting spandex outfit was very sexy. Maybe that's why Spice Girl Victoria Beckham also chose to wear one. She appeared in a catsuit for several of her music videos.

Soon the catsuit became popular, but that popularity was short-lived. Made of latex, PVC, or spandex, it was worn with high-heeled boots. It wasn't a practical look for most women.

Another trendy one-piece outfit was overalls. This farm garment made a comeback in the 1990s. Overalls were especially popular with teenagers. They liked to wear them with one strap undone or with both straps down

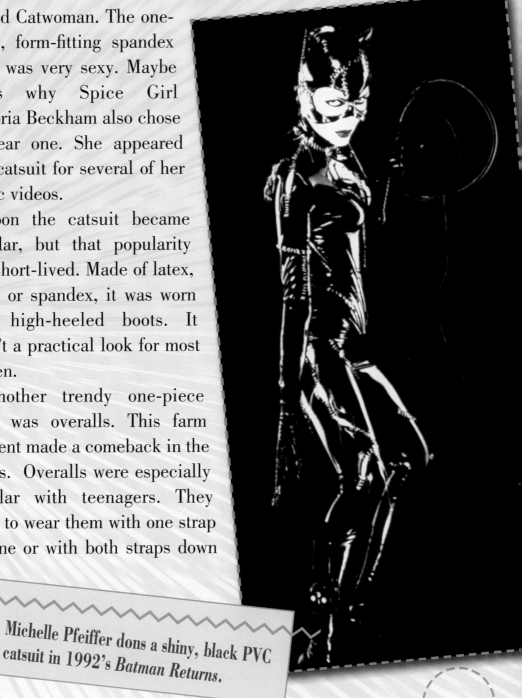

Michelle Pfeiffer dons a shiny, black PVC catsuit in 1992's *Batman Returns*.

1

A denim overall dress with one strap undone from 1997. This type of sleeveless dress that you fasten on is also called a jumper.

Actress Sara Gilbert played Darlene Conner in the sitcom *Roseanne* from 1988 to 1997. Her character dressed in tomboyish, grungy clothing that included ripped jeans and flannel shirts.

and a belt holding them up. Today, you're more likely to see overalls in children's wardrobes or on the farm.

Of course, in the nineties, people were paying for jeans that already looked worn. The jeans were ripped on purpose. Some were bleached and faded. The "distressed" look was very popular. Jeans also got a new material. Designers added Lycra®. This allowed the denim to stretch a bit.

These were just some of the fun fads during the nineties. But the 1990s were more than just fads. Read on to find out more.

Hairstyles

In the 1990s, hair was all about natural beauty. Women were too busy with work, school, and their families to fuss with their hair. They wanted more low-maintenance hairstyles. They asked for cuts that matched their face shapes and individual styles.

Ideas came from television and movies. On the TV show *Friends,* one of the actresses had a new style that women wanted to copy. On the medical drama *ER,* one of the actors had a popular haircut that many men copied.

Some of these hairstyles appeared for the very first time during this decade. Others were updates of earlier styles. For example, the bob hairstyle was first popular in the 1920s. In the 1990s, new updated bobs were everywhere.

Hairstyles

You could wear your hair curly or straight in the 1990s. You could even wear it crimped. Crimped hair had regular ridges or folds, similar to the waves worn back in the 1920s. But unlike earlier decades when crimped hair was short and neat, the new modern look was often seen on medium to long hair. Women crimped their hair with crimping irons. They sometimes left it long or pinned part of it up.

Many men kept their hair short and well groomed during this time. Some shaved their heads, perhaps inspired by celebrities such as basketball player Michael Jordan. Others wore long sideburns, which were a throwback to the sixties and seventies. Special shampoos and grooming products for men were becoming more common on the shelves.

The Rachel

One of the most popular cuts of the 1990s was a combination of styles. It was a little curly and a little straight. It was shoulder length but had short pieces, too. It was golden brown and a bit blonde. It was the Rachel!

The Rachel was named after a TV character on the popular sitcom *Friends*. The show was one of the most widely watched programs at the time. The Rachel was the layered cut that actress Jennifer Aniston wore—and that many women tried to copy—in the 1990s.

Jennifer Aniston sports the iconic Rachel haircut on the second season of Friends.

Love Those Layers!

Layers were not just seen on the Rachel cut. They were everywhere! One hairstyle could have many different lengths. And there wasn't just one type of layered look. You could layer any part of your hair, or all of it. Actress Meg Ryan wore her short blonde hair in a cute layered cut.

Hairstyles

Model Kathy Ireland wore her brunette hair in long, luxurious layers.

Layers naturally add body to hair. If you have a natural curl, you would see it in your layered cut. If you have really thick, heavy hair, the layers would also let it flow more easily.

What About Bob?

You probably have seen the bob. It is a short haircut that falls just below your ears. It could be cut straight across. It also could be angled so the front is a little longer than the back. Bobs can be worn with or without bangs.

Supermodel Linda Evangelista wore a bob in the 1990s. She wore one again in 2007. It is one of those classic styles that seem to always be in fashion.

Linda Evangelista wore a sleek bob with bangs and a diagonal part in 1996.

In the 1990s, some women even made this classic cut a little funky. They wore an asymmetrical bob, where one side was a different length than the other. This was especially popular among punk rockers.

Hail to the Caesar!

With men, the ultrashort Caesar cut was popular. It was named after the Roman general Julius Caesar because it looked like the cut he wore. You could recognize it by its short bangs. The rest of the hair was also fairly short, about an inch or two around the head.

It was a style that looked boyish, especially on mature men. Actor George Clooney on the TV show *ER* helped make the style popular. It is still considered a good style for men today.

George Clooney's Caesar haircut in the mid-nineties.

Chapter 2
Women's Styles and Fashion

Was there anything really new in the 1990s? It seemed that many designers recycled ideas from other decades. In this way, they gave retro clothing—styles that are about twenty or twenty-five years old—a fresh new feel.

One example of retro fashion was the baby doll style. It first appeared as pajamas in the 1950s and in the next decades as dresses. Baby doll dresses and blouses came back again in the 1990s. You can still see them today.

Low-rise jeans were just a modern version of the 1970s hip-hugger. Waistlines moved higher in the eighties and back down again in the nineties.

Going Back in Time

In the 1990s, the styles of the sixties, seventies, and eighties were hot again. Retro fashion was the rage. Women went to vintage clothing stores. They pulled old pieces from their closets. They put together looks that were part of the past.

Plenty of people followed this trend. On TV, *That '70s Show* featured the platform shoes and wide collars that people copied in the nineties. There were also celebrities who wore retro looks. These included actresses Renée Zellweger and Julia Roberts and model Kate Moss.

The New Jean

Look at the button of your jeans. If it's above your belly button, you're wearing a high-rise jean. If it's below, it's a low-rise. Low-rise jeans became popular in the 1990s and into the 2000s. At first, they were tight with a straight-leg fit. Later, low-rise jeans came in flare leg and baggy styles. Stonewashed styles were also popular.

The Baby Doll Look

Baby doll dresses feature waistlines that come up high, under the bust. The skirts flare out. They are usually fairly short, emphasizing the legs. The baby doll blouse has a similar shape. It just ends shorter and is worn over pants or shorts. The movie *Clueless* showed baby doll dresses with puffed sleeves. They were worn with thigh-high stockings.

Supermodel Tyra Banks wore low-rise jeans and a cropped top to a 1997 charity event.

Jason Priestley and Shannen Doherty played brother and sister in the wildly popular teen drama *Beverly Hills, 90210,* which ran from 1990 to 2000. Doherty is wearing a baby doll dress with boots, adding a bohemian touch.

Spaghetti Strap Tank

By the late 1990s, women had discovered the spaghetti strap tank. This was a tight-fitting tank top with thin straps. It was a more feminine version of the original tank top with its wider straps. Spaghetti strap tanks could be worn alone or layered over or under clothes. They continue to be popular today.

Academy Award–winning actress Halle Berry keeps it cool and simple in a white spaghetti strap tank top.

Chapter 3

Men's Styles and Fashion

Men found their casual style in the 1990s, with more choices than ever before. There were the comfortable and practical cargo pants, which were styled after workmen's pants. There were also baggy jeans, the style worn by hip-hop artists, and T-shirts with bold logos.

Leather jackets for men have been around for decades. The 1990s took this popular style and updated it with a new length and new colors.

Casual wear got a lot of use, especially as workplaces began to offer "casual Fridays" or dress-down days. Men still had to look professional, but it was easy to put together a nice look. There were many choices in the nineties.

Cargo Pants

You may have seen work pants like carpenter's or painter's pants. They have a lot of large pockets where workers can keep their tools. Cargo pants were inspired by them. They are a more stylish version of work pants.

Cargo pants were named because of the cargo they could carry. They have several large and deep pockets in the front and the back. Most close with buttons, snaps, or Velcro. Usually beige or khaki colored, cargo pants are often made of cotton. They can also come in other fabrics and colors.

Baggy Jeans

It was stylish in the 1990s to wear baggy jeans. Often, this look was taken to the extreme. Young men wore jeans that were several sizes too big. The result was jeans that would practically fall off them. You could see the upper band of their underwear.

Cargo pants were available as shorts in the summer.

The young boys to the left and middle dress in baggy jeans and oversize shirts. The hip-hop style was especially popular in urban areas.

There are a couple of theories about why big and baggy pants were popular. Some say it came from poor families handing down pants that were too big. Others say it was similar to a prison uniform, which was too baggy to fit well. Still others credit the fashion to skateboarders who wanted freedom of movement.

But whatever the reason, designers took note. Tommy Hilfiger created a line of baggy denim. The Gap and Old Navy did, too. Levi's was slow to do so, and, as a result, the brand saw a drop in sales.

Loving That Leather

Leather jackets have been around for a long time. The 1950s, for example, featured a lot of leather bomber jackets typically worn by men. In the 1990s, the leather jacket was restyled in new shapes, lengths, and colors. The longer three-quarter-length leather trench coat became popular. Worn by such action hero actors as Steven Seagal, it reached mid-thigh. Keanu Reeves wore a similar style in the 1999 science-fiction film *The Matrix*.

Actor Brad Pitt took the style to a new level in his movie *Fight Club*. His red leather jacket inspired men to play with color.

The popular boy band *NSYNC (pronounced "in sink") attend the 1999 Billboard Awards in matching leather jackets.

23

Under the Suit

Until the 1990s, the traditional male work "uniform" was a dark suit and a button-down shirt. The shirt was typically in white or off-white, with the tie lending some color.

But that began to change as men took note of the more casual looks in mass media. They still wore some version of the blue, black, or gray suit. But they wore dress shirts without ties. Some wore sweater vests under their jackets. Or they wore button-down shirts in pastel or bright colors.

As some offices offered casual dress-down days, men reached into their closets for classic looks from past decades, including T-shirts, jackets, and khaki pants or jeans.

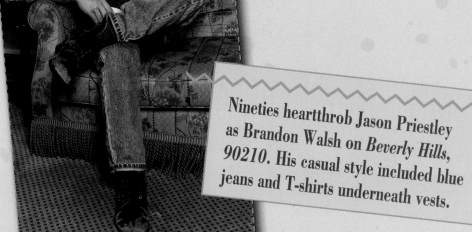

Nineties heartthrob Jason Priestley as Brandon Walsh on *Beverly Hills, 90210*. His casual style included blue jeans and T-shirts underneath vests.

Chapter 4

Accessories

By now, you know a lot about 1990s fashion. All you need to complete your nineties look is a lesson on accessories.

First, a "must" in your nineties closet would be the pashmina. This popular wrap appeared in the mid-1990s, and it's still around. The soft shawl immediately brightens the style of any outfit. Maybe its popularity is due to the fact that it can be used in so many ways.

Another item you would have in your closet would be leggings. These formfitting leg coverings would take the place of pants. If you were young, you might also own a pair of thigh-high stockings. Both the leggings and the stockings worked well with the short skirts of the time.

Don't forget the shoes. In the 1990s, retro styles were popular. But they weren't the same old shoes we saw in the fifties, sixties, or seventies. New technology gave us new materials. Designers also added a modern take.

Finally, you might have a piercing or two. In the 1990s, body piercing became more common. It was not just for punk rockers anymore.

Body Piercing

Pierced ears were just the beginning of piercing in the nineties. Body piercing became more commonplace around this time. Piercing was especially popular among young people. You didn't have to be part of the punk movement. Both men and women did it. They could have several holes pierced in their ears. They pierced their eyebrows and tongues. Women pierced their bellybuttons. It was a way to attract attention.

In most places, if you are under eighteen, you need your parents' permission in order to get a piercing.

Body piercings, like tattoos, are a form of self-expression.

26

It is also very important to make sure that the place where you are getting pierced uses sterilized tools. Otherwise, you could get a painful infection.

The Pashmina

The pashmina wrap dates back to ancient Persia. The word *pashm* refers to the softest underhair on the belly of a goat. In ancient times, only royalty or wealthy people could afford a wrap made of pashm.

In the 1990s, the pashmina made its appearance in America. Its soft, silky feel made it popular. Women wore it as a shawl, sash, scarf, and even belt. The colored pashminas brightened outfits. They were used to add color to neutrals, such as when they were worn over winter coats.

A wide selection of brightly colored pashminas on display in a bazaar.

Love Those Legs!

Leggings are comfortable and stylish. Made of cotton and Lycra, a spandex synthetic fiber, leggings stretch easily and offer a tight fit. Leggings are like tights, but they end at the ankle. In the 1990s, teenagers would wear them under short skirts. Women wore them with long sweaters or tops.

Teens also wore thigh-high stockings. The stockings went over the knee and were worn with short skirts. The two popular colors were very basic: black and white.

American actress Christina Ricci sports a skirt and leggings combo in 1991.

The New "Old" Shoes

Everything old was new again. At least that's how it was with 1990s shoe styles. Designers took some popular old trends and used new materials. The result was a wide range of choices in trendy footwear.

The platform shoe was back. But it wasn't the chunky clog or cork sole we saw in the 1970s. It was a stylish wedge like the sequined dress shoes Madonna wore, done in satin by Dolce and Gabbana.

Some men and women went back to nature. They wore sensible styles like Birkenstock® sandals and Hush Puppies®, once associated with the hippie generation.

These patent leather shoes combine elements from many different types of shoes. Overall they look like Mary Janes, but they have platform soles, high heels, and two straps across the instep.

29

Finally, sneakers became very fashionable. In fact, some of them weren't designed for exercise at all. The Reebok Nobok had a high heel. The flat-bottomed plimsoll became a popular street style.

Hip-hop artist Puff Daddy (also known as P. Diddy) attends the 1998 MTV Movie Awards in all white. In the nineties, sneakers became acceptable footwear for special events.

Chapter 5

Fads and Trends

You have your own personal style. So did people in the 1990s. Some were more outrageous than others.

Take grunge, for example. If you wanted to look like you did not care about fashion, you might consider grunge. It was certainly easier to get ready in the morning when you did not need to do your hair or iron your clothes.

But that sloppy look wasn't for everyone. It definitely wasn't worn by everyone. Just a small group of young people adopted the grunge look.

Then there was goth, a dark and mysterious fashion. Again, it was popular among some young people. But not everyone adopted this look either.

Eco fashion may be a little easier to understand. This is fashion that is good for the environment.

People learned that they could be fashionable while still protecting their planet and values.

Perhaps the strangest fad in the 1990s was one inspired by two hip-hop artists. This group wore their clothes backward. Believe it or not, as a result, so did others.

Grunge

You probably don't look like you just rolled out of bed. But people who followed the grunge movement did. They were rebelling against the yuppie look of the eighties. So they wore an anti-fashion look. It included ripped jeans, clunky boots, and plaid flannel shirts. Messy hair was often part of the look.

Nirvana was the most popular grunge band of the 1990s.

The grunge look began in Seattle, Washington. That's where grunge music, a type of hard rock, became popular. Musicians and their fans sported the grunge look.

Going Goth

In the 1970s, it wasn't unusual to see people going goth. Two decades later, in the 1990s, it became fashionable again. "Goth" is short for the gothic look. It was a dark and spooky look that almost resembled that of a vampire.

Dyed black hair, dark eyeliner, and black fingernails were all part of the goth look. Goths also dressed mostly in black. Goth fashion sometimes featured metal studs or spokes. Sometimes, Victorian corsets and waistcoats were part of the look.

American actress Fairuza Balk sports the goth look in the 1996 film *The Craft*. Note the black hair and clothing, cross earrings, spiked collar, and blood-red lipstick.

People who were goth usually had many piercings. They often wore extreme haircuts, such as mohawks or dreadlocks. The result was very dramatic.

Eco Fashion

There was a growing concern for the environment in the 1990s. That had people looking for fabric fibers that were

grown without pesticides. They also wanted dyes that would not hurt the environment. The result was eco fashion.

The goal of eco fashion is to protect our planet's resources. That means that people not only grow materials responsibly but use them for more than one season. They also pay for the clothes fairly. They don't take advantage of low prices in factories in faraway countries.

A model struts on the runway in a linen dress and a straw hat, fashion pieces made out of natural fibers.

Eco fashion has grown since the 1990s. In the 2000s, many organic materials are being used to make clothing. Bamboo, organically grown and dyed cotton, and other materials have been introduced as eco-friendly.

Dressing Backward

In the nineties, hip-hop music was becoming more popular. It was a type of rap music. Early hip-hop artists included a group called Kriss Kross, also known as Chris Kelly and Chris Smith. They were known as much for their music as for a particular fashion statement that they made. They wore their clothes backward.

Their peculiar style was a way to highlight their name. The group's producer did a lot of publicity around it. The interesting thing was that it caught on! Kids started wearing their pants and shirts backward to school. There are even annual Kriss Kross days when people dress backward to honor the pair.

Hip-hop duo Kriss Kross wore their pants backward.

Chapter 6

Pop Culture

The world seemed to be getting smaller through-out the twentieth century. New technology, from telephones to televisions, brought information right to your doorstep. In the 1990s, it really started shrinking. It became easier to communicate with people all over the world.

One way was by computer. People "surfed" the Internet for news, games, and information about a variety of topics. You could find out what was happening in your state or in a country halfway around the world. You also could have conversations by e-mail or instant message.

Another way to communicate was by cell phone. For the first time, you could be reached almost anywhere you were. All you needed was a cell-phone tower to transmit the signal.

Technology affected our lives in other ways, too. It led the way for reality TV. Until then, unscripted TV programs usually had secret cameras that filmed people. Now they were publicly filming real people living their lives.

Hand-held video games also were popular during this time. It was like having a video arcade right at home. Games from such companies as Nintendo were on the wish list for many children during the 1990s.

These new technologies really changed the way we live. It's hard to imagine life without them!

The Cell-Phone Epidemic

Today, you can't go anywhere without seeing someone on a cell phone. But before the 1990s, cell phones were not that common. Wireless technology was just being developed. Even cordless phones were relatively new. The first cell phones appeared in the eighties.

The difference between cordless phones and cellular phones was that cordless phones only worked close to the base where they were charged.

Early cell phones were heavy and bulky, and they could only be used to talk.

Cellular phones could work anywhere there was a wireless signal. That meant that for the first time, people could be reached almost anywhere they happened to be.

In 1983, a cell phone cost $3,500 and weighed a pound. There was no texting, video, or cameras. But in the 1990s, that all changed. Cell-phone prices came down. Phones became smaller and did more. Today, it is estimated that more people have cell phones than have landlines.

The Internet

Can you imagine a world without computers? How about a world without the World Wide Web? It was not that long ago that that was the case. Personal computers first appeared in the late seventies. They became more common in homes in the 1980s. Computer scientists had experimented with sending electronic messages. In 1989, the first e-mail system was connected through the Ohio State University network. But it wasn't really public yet.

In 1991, a man named Tim Berners-Lee introduced the World Wide Web as a way for people to share information. He used a format in which you could see documents on your screen without downloading them to your computer. Another inventor, Marc Andreessen, invented the first Internet browser, called Mosaic, in 1993. Then AOL launched its e-mail system. Finally, anyone could get an e-mail address. That was the start of the Internet as we know it today.

Before laptops and smart phones, there were desktop computers. There are still desktop computers today, but they are much sleeker and smaller and have flat-screen monitors.

As more people got personal computers, they started using the Internet. It was a way to communicate with family, friends, and business people. It was a way to find out information. By 1996, there were about 45 million users. By 1999, there were 150 million.

Tune Into Reality TV

In 1992, MTV introduced a new TV show called *The Real World*, which followed the lives of seven strangers who shared a house for several months. Rather than scripting the show, the cable network decided that putting different types of people together would create enough drama.

This was a completely new approach to television. Up until then, you could have a show that wasn't scripted, but it was probably a game show or one where there was a hidden camera to catch people's reactions in different situations.

The first season of *The Real World* had seven housemates and a dog named Gouda. MTV's groundbreaking program paved the way for all the reality shows that followed, such as *Survivor* and *The Jersey Shore*.

The Real World was the beginning of reality TV as we know it today. Footage shot at the house was edited down to weekly episodes. Housemates dealt with issues ranging from prejudice to religion to romance. People tuned in.

The first *Real World* took place in New York. Each season, the producers move the location. In the 1990s, there were *Real World* shows in Los Angeles, San Francisco, London, and Hawaii. In 2011, *The Real World* returned to Las Vegas for its twenty-fifth season.

Nintendo

Chances are there is a home video game system in your house. Or you might own a handheld version. Nintendo was the company that helped make the handheld console popular, and it happened during the 1990s.

Video games had been around since the 1970s. The early games were played using machines that hooked up to your TV. Some of the first handheld devices were introduced by the end of the decade. But they were simple machines with dots or lines for graphics.

Then it happened. Gunpei Yokoi was traveling on a train one day. He noticed a bored businessman playing with his calculator. A game designer for Nintendo, Yokoi saw an opportunity. He thought he could create a watch that also had games on it. It would sell well to bored businessmen.

That was the beginning of something great. Nintendo used the technology in tiny calculators to create games. Then, the company combined that with the technology used to play games on a TV. The result was the Game Boy, launched in 1989.

Because of its low price, its interesting games, and long battery life, the Game Boy became a best seller during the 1990s. It helped that there were such games as *Super Mario World, The Legend of Zelda: A Link to the Past, Street Fighter II,* and the *Final Fantasy* series.

Teenagers play with Game Boys at an electronics fair in Germany in 1997.

In 1996, Nintendo launched a smaller, lighter version called the Game Boy Pocket, which still had the original's green monochromatic screen. Two years later, the Game Boy Color came out. Gamers could finally view their favorite digital worlds and characters in color. Game Boy, still popular today, has led the way for many other devices. Now, there's no reason to be bored!

Timeline

The 1920s

The look: cloche hats, dropped-waist dresses, long strands of pearls (women), and baggy pants (men)

The hair: short bobs

The fad: raccoon coats

The 1930s

The look: dropped hemlines, natural waists, practical shoes (women), and blazers and trousers (men)

The hair: finger waves and permanents

The fad: sunbathing

The 1940s

The look: shirtwaist dresses and military style (women) and suits and fedoras (men)

The hair: victory rolls and updos

The fad: kangaroo cloaks

The 1950s

The look: circular skirts and saddle shoes (women) and the greaser look (men)

The hair: bouffants and pompadours

The fad: coonskin hats

The 1960s

The look: bell-bottoms and miniskirts (women) and turtlenecks and hipster pants (men)

The hair: beehives and pageboys

The fad: go-go boots

The 1970s

The look: designer jeans (women) and leisure suits (men)

The hair: shags and Afros

The fad: hot pants

The 1980s

The look: preppy (women and men) and *Miami Vice* (men)

The hair: side ponytails and mullets

The fad: ripped off-the-shoulder sweatshirts

The 1990s

The look: low-rise, straight-leg jeans (both women and men)

The hair: the "Rachel" cut from *Friends*

The fad: ripped, acid-washed jeans

The 2000s

The look: leggings and long tunic tops (women) and the sophisticated urban look (men)

The hair: feminine, face-framing cuts (with straight hair dominating over curly)

The fad: organic and bamboo clothing

Glossary

accessories—Items that are worn in addition to clothing, such as jewelry, gloves, hats, and belts.

Birkenstock—A brand of sandals.

bob—A woman's short haircut, which hangs below the ears.

catsuit—A skintight bodysuit for a woman.

crimped—Styled in small waves or ridges.

dramatic—Theatrical, easily noticed.

fad—A craze that happens for a brief period of time.

fashion—The current style of dressing.

Hush Puppies—A brand of casual footwear.

latex—A man-made rubber.

leggings—Footless tights.

Lycra—The brand name for a type of spandex.

organic—Grown or raised without drugs, hormones, or chemicals.

overalls—A one-piece garment with a front panel and shoulder straps.

pashmina—A shawl.

pigment—A substance that is used to color something.

PVC—A type of vinyl that is commonly used to make rainwear.

retro—Referring to the past.

sitcom—A TV show known as a situation comedy.

spandex—A stretchy man-made fabric.

stonewashed—Processed to appear worn-out.

trend—The general direction in which things are heading.

yuppie—The nickname for the young urban or upwardly mobile professional.

Further Reading

Books

Jones, Jen. *Fashion History: Looking Great Through the Ages.* Mankato, Minn.: Capstone Press, 2007.

McEvoy, Anne. *Fashions of a Decade: The 1990s.* New York: Infobase Publishing, 2007.

Rooney, Anne. *The 1990s.* Mankato, Minn.: Arcturus Publishing, 2010.

Steer, Deirdre Clancy. *The 1980s and 1990s.* New York: Chelsea House, 2009.

Internet Addresses

Fashion-Era: "1990s Fashion History"
<http://www.fashion-era.com/the_1990s.htm>

Kidzworld: "'90s Fashion Trends"
<http://www.kidzworld.com/article/4632-90s-fashion-trends>

Index